Ping-Pong

by Michèle Dufresne

Literacy Footprints, Inc.

Ping-pong is a fun game.

Ping-pong is a game like tennis.

In tennis, you hit the ball over a net.

In ping-pong, you hit
the ball over a net, too.

You play ping-pong
on a big table.

Here is a ping-pong ball
and a paddle.

The player hits the ball
with the paddle.

The game is fast.

The ball goes up.

The ball goes down.

The ball goes fast, and
it can spin.

Ping-pong is a fun game!

Ping-Pong

ball

ne

paddle

tabl

tenni